ABE
LINCOLN
AFLOAT

J. C. Ladenheim

HERITAGE BOOKS
2008

HERITAGE BOOKS
AN IMPRINT OF HERITAGE BOOKS, INC.

Books, CDs, and more—Worldwide

For our listing of thousands of titles see our website
at
www.HeritageBooks.com

Published 2008 by
HERITAGE BOOKS, INC.
Publishing Division
100 Railroad Ave. #104
Westminster, Maryland 21157

Other books by the author:

Alien Horseman: An Italian Shavetail with Custer

Custer's Thorn: The Life of Frederick W. Benteen

The Jarrett-Palmer Express of 1876: Coast to Coast in Eighty-three Hours

International Standard Book Numbers
Paperbound: 978-0-7884-4558-3
Clothbound: 978-0-7884-7165-0

INTRODUCTION

Some 35,000 books have been written about the life of Abraham Lincoln. In them, the reader finds surprisingly few details of the two roundtrip journeys Lincoln made to New Orleans. These omissions are all the more curious, since the travels accounted for a half year of Lincoln's formative life and occurred at a time when he was passing into early manhood. So enthralled was Lincoln with his experiences on the river that he explored the possibility of embarking on a steamboat career; but was thwarted by his age and parental obligations. Nevertheless, he acquired the reputation of a competent riverboat man, and even secured brief employment as a riverboat pilot.

Accordingly, the author feels justified in more fully describing those voyages and collating them with the experiences and reports of contemporary travelers. In order to orient the reader, I have presented a brief narrative of Lincoln's early life, the details of which have been arbitrarily selected, so as not to embroil the reader in controversy beyond the scope of this study.

The librarians of the Manuscript Room and the Genealogy and History Room of the New York Public Library were most helpful to me, and I use this occasion to thank them for their kind assistance. Jane E. Gastineaux made available the invaluable resources of the Lincoln Museum of Ft. Wayne. Roxanne Carlson was my esteemed editor, to whom I am profoundly grateful. Mrs. Jean Ganley relieved me of many bothers so that I could undertake this study.

Abe Lincoln Afloat

THE LINCOLN FAMILY reached the shores of Massachusetts in 1637, seventeen years after the Pilgrims landed, and in five successive generations spread south through New Jersey and Pennsylvania to Virginia. Often, the eldest son remained on the holding and the younger departed, in quest of promising opportunities elsewhere. Abraham Lincoln, grandfather of the future President, left Virginia in 1782 and made his way with Daniel Boone through the Cumberland Pass and along the Wilderness Trail into Kentucky. He took with him a wife, three sons and two daughters. Two of the older sons are said to have been born to a first wife (Mary Shipley), who died in Virginia; the youngest son, Thomas, was born to his second (?) wife (Bathsheba Herrin).[1]

The family settled in western Kentucky on the Licking Creek, twenty miles from Fort Beargrass, (later Louisville); where Grandfather Abraham laid claim to 500 acres. A few years later, he was killed by Indians. Thomas was then six years old. Apparently the two older sons and their step (?) mother were not on cordial terms, for she left the cabin and went with Thomas and a young sister to live elsewhere. Tom Lincoln was raised partly by his mother and partly by kin. From early age, he was hired out to earn money. As he grew older, he acquired the skills of a backwoods farmer and

---

[1] Barton maintains that he had only one wife, Bathsheba. William E. Barton, *The Life of Abraham Lincoln,* 27 et seq.

hunter. With money he had earned (or perhaps with money obtained from a patrimony), he purchased raw land, but it is doubtful that he farmed it extensively, since a homestead required a woman, and he had not yet married. Later, from a Joseph Hanks in Elizabethtown, Kentucky, he learned the craft of a carpenter/cabinet maker.

In 1806, Thomas Lincoln was hired to build a flatboat, which he and an Isaac Bush sailed down the Ohio and Mississippi Rivers to New Orleans. It may not have been Tom's first visit. In those days, the danger of river pirates made the journey especially hazardous. Most brazen of all, were the robbers that infested the Illinois wilderness near what was called "Cave-in-Rock." They lay in wait for the unsuspecting boatmen, murdered them and stole their cargo.

Settlements were infrequent along the banks of the Ohio and Mississippi, and there were few inducements to stop during the trip before Louisiana was reached.

New Orleans was the final destination, the Zion of Splendors. Situated 125 miles up from the Gulf of Mexico, it was the lifeblood of the whole trans-Appalachian region, through which were funneled the produce of the Ohio Valley and the furs, minerals and the surplus crops from the upper Mississippi. Three-eighths of the entire agricultural production of the United States passed through New Orleans.

Founded in 1718 by the French, and named for the Duke of Orleans (later Louis XV), the settlement was inundated in 1719, but repopulated three years later. During their almost half-century of occupation, the French had left a firm imprint on the Louisiana Territory extending up to the Great Lakes. In 1762, France ceded Louisiana to Spain, to compensate it for joining with them in the French and Indian War. Once in possession, Spain made repeated attempts to extend its hegemony over the American settlers of trans-Appalachia, who were completely dependant on New Orleans for the sale of their agricultural surplus. For a while, Spain closed the port to the Americans and denied them the "right of deposit," but was persuaded to reopen the city in 1795, after American settlers threatened to invade it. In 1802, Spain secretly returned New Orleans and the Louisiana Territory to France, in return for "considerations." First Consul Napoleon Bonaparte promptly closed the port and threatened American interests. However, before he could dispatch troops to the Mississippi Valley, his army in Haiti suffered defeat in battle and by yellow fever. Rather than risk certain loss of the Louisiana Territory in the forthcoming war with Great Britain, Bonaparte sold it to the United States.

With New Orleans in American hands, commerce was revitalized. Within five years, two thousand flatboats annually descended on New Orleans, bringing to it a cargo worth five million dollars.[2] By the time of Thomas's visit, the population of the city had grown to twenty thousand. For the backwoods Kentucky settler, New Orleans would be his very first encounter with city life. Tom Lincoln may have previously visited Louisville, Kentucky, but Louisville then had a population of only one thousand, four hundred.

The flatboat man could return home by land or by river. Several kinds of upriver craft gave employment to boatmen in pre-steamboat times. *Keelboats* were named for their long timber keel, which cleaved the water. They were pointed fore and aft,[3] had a ribbed hull with planking, a draft of twenty to sixty inches, a length of thirty to seventy-five feet, a beam of five to ten feet and carried a burden of twenty to forty tons.[4]

---

[2] Charles H. Ambler, *A History of Transportation in the Ohio Valley*, 72.

[3] Donald Davidson, *The Rivers of America*, Vol. 1, 207.

[4] Leland Johnson, *Falls City Engineers*, Chap. 2, *Ohio River Navigation,* 27, in http://www.usace.army.mil/publications/misc/un22/toc.htm

Barges were keelboats with overhead enclosures, which sometimes rigged sail. *Packetboats* were large barges that carried passengers. *Bateaux* were skiff-like longboats, moved by several sets of oars, but these craft were obsolete. They had been used by the French to carry a few important passengers and the mail. When on a military mission, the bateau mounted a small scatter cannon.

The keelboat, barge and packetboat moved upriver by poling. Half the crew stood on the right side, the other half on the left.[5] Each crewmember would set his iron-trimmed pole in the shallow water at the bow and walk over a cleated runway to the stern, propelling the craft forward. If the river bottom was too deep or too soft, then "cordelling" was employed. The crew would attach a one-hundred-yard-long warping line to the boat and wind it around a tree and reeve it through a block and tackle, to winch the boat forward.[6] When the boat was near the shore, the crew could move it by tugging on bushes ("bush whacking").[7]

The keelboat traveled upriver no faster than one mile an hour. Six miles progress was a good day's work. As many as fourteen men might man a keelboat, sometimes more. For the four months of travel between New Orleans to Louisville, each crewmember received seventy-five dollars and a generous allowance of whiskey. Such a trip might cost the owner $1,750, but he could expect to net $1,500.[8] Favorite cargos for upriver transport were coffee, tea, sugar and molasses, since they do not spoil.[9]

---

[5] On the inland waterways, the terms "port" and "starboard" are discouraged.
[6] Robert Riegel and Robert Athearn, *America Moves West,* 220.
[7] Willard Price, *The Amazing Mississippi*, 54.
[8] Johnson, *The Falls River Navigation*, 29.
[9] Ibid., 30.

The keelboat crew was a special breed of mostly professional boatmen, selected for their strength and endurance. Anyone applying for a one-way job would not have been warmly received, nor were his prospects of employment favorable.

Tom Lincoln and his companion returned home on "shank's mare," as walking was called. They traveled by road from New Orleans to Natchez, and then, from Natchez to Nashville, by the 450-mile Natchez Trace, also known as "the old Chickasaw Trail" or "the Bloody Path." Almost everyone going north took this trail. It was part of the adventure and the worst part of the trip.[10]

The trail was first authorized for white travelers in 1801 by treaty with the Cherokee, Chickasaw and Choctaw Nations, through whose land the trail passed. Before the coming of the steamboat, thousands of people walked the trail each month. The path was eight feet wide, and by 1809 a wagon could pass with difficulty. Most men went on foot and used their horses, if they had any, as pack animals.[11] There were few improvements along the way, apart from the huts ("stands") operated by the Chickasaw and Choctaw traders, which provided shelter for the night. Travelers stepped from stone to stone over bogs, crossed rivers over fallen logs and swam the horses.[12] The lower half of the trace was swampy and went through Choctaw lands; the upper half was hilly and traversed Chickasaw domain. The Nations were generally friendly, with exceptions, but horses had to be carefully guarded at nighttime.[13] Wolves, bears, mosquitoes and poison ivy were to

---

[10] Davidson, *The Rivers of America*, Vol. 1, 215.

[11] Ibid., 215.

[12] Pedkop Bambera, *The Natches Trace*, 3, in http://www.texaschapbookpress.com/sites.htm

[13] Davidson, *The Rivers of America*, Vol. 1, 216.

be feared. Highwaymen ("land pirates") gave especial concern. Lurid stories were told of robbers who murdered the traveler, filled his cavities with stones and sank the corpse in a creek. The worst of all bandits, however, were those who infested the waterfront in Natchez-under-the Hill, ever ready to rob and kill the redoubtable flatboat man.

Upon his return, Tom Lincoln credited his pay of sixteen pounds (gold) to his running account with a local merchant, in anticipation of the expenses of his forthcoming marriage.

In June 1806, a month after his return from New Orleans, Thomas Lincoln, then twenty-eight, married the twenty-three-year-old Nancy Hanks. The marriage had to draw on Tom's assets, since Nancy came with no dowry. She was born in Virginia, the daughter of Lucy Hanks, an unwed mother, and an unknown father. Lucy took the baby girl to Kentucky and handed her over to an aunt for rearing. Near the home of Nancy's foster parents was the cabin of Bathsheba Lincoln, so it is certain that Tom had known Nancy for many years. The newlyweds lived briefly in the hamlet of Elizabethtown, where their first child, Sarah, was born.

Kentucky was then immersed in a pervasive land boom. The goal for most men was to acquire as much land as they could come by, since land was a man's measure. As mentioned, in 1803, Tom had bought raw land at Mill Creek, eight miles north of Elizabethtown, whether for speculation, for light farming or for future use is unsettled. The land turned out to be unprofitable, partly because of a defect in the title. Now that he was married, Tom was ready to try his hand at homesteading. His first effort proved to be a disaster. The land he "purchased" at Nolin Creek, eighteen miles southeast of Elizabethtown, turned out to have poor soil and defective title; or rather, no title at all.

Title in Kentucky was often dubious. Some settlers squatted ("cornpatch and cabin"), hoping later to acquire title. Others bought land heedless of the title's quality. Some acquired warrants, which allowed them to own land, but required that before title was issued, that the land be surveyed and registered.[14] Surveys were primitive and frequently based on impermanent markers. Natural landmarks were not always available; rivers changed courses. Often, the survey began with initials carved into a tree trunk and burnished with gunpowder. Measurements were taken in rods or poles.

Plats overlapped, sometimes even with the surveyor's knowledge. Since land registers were overworked, many a settler never bothered to register his claim, especially if he had doubts about its validity. Lawsuits were legion and provided profitable employment for droves of newly arrived lawyers. Daniel Boone held claims for 100,000 acres[15] and ended up landless, as did most of the first generation of Kentucky frontiersmen. Tom's bitterness toward land lawyers may have been reflected in the later writings of his son: "Who can be more nearly a fiend than he who habitually overhauls [inspects] the register of deeds in search of defects in titles, whereon to stir up strife and put money in his pocket?"[16]

It was during the sojourn on the Nolin Creek farm, that Abraham was born, on a bed of poles covered with corn husks. After two years of unproductive labor, Thomas abandoned his first homestead and moved to the Knob Creek Farm, seven miles away. The land had better soil and better prospects, since it lay on the Nashville-Louisville road. At the

---

[14] Davidson, *Rivers of America*, Vol. 1, 213; also Thomas Clark, *Frontier America*, 136.

[15] John Mack Faragher, *Daniel Boone*, 245.

[16] "Notes for a Law Lecture, July1, 1850[?]," [ed] Philip Van Doren Stern, *The Life and Writings of Abraham Lincoln*, 327.

appropriate time, he sent his two children to subscription schools, where they learned their letters and ciphers.

Thomas is said to have early displayed a dislike for slavery, which was becoming more prevalent in Hardin County, where Elizabethtown and all three of his holdings at one time were located. His upland forebears had a long-standing hatred of the large plantation owners, who controlled the state legislatures in Virginia and North Carolina and had imposed burdensome taxes on the poor white settler. Their resentment led to the bloody "Regulator Rebellion,"[17] which was violently suppressed; but the struggle engendered a bitterness that was passed down to succeeding generations.

Tom's hostility was directed primarily toward the plantation owner. It does not necessarily follow, however, that he had concern for the slave. Like most settlers, he feared the slave would diminish the ability of the poor white to support himself. Tom had once served as a "night patroller," whose duties included the capture and whippings of slaves found wandering at night without permission from their owner. On the other hand, he and Nancy were married by a preacher who was a fiery opponent of slavery. Moreover, Tom worshiped with a Baptist denomination that vigorously opposed slavery. Each Baptist church had autonomy to formulate its own attitude toward slavery.

After five productive years spent on the Knob Creek farm, Tom was once again immersed in title difficulties, when an ejection suit was brought against him. It turned out that some woman back East held title to a huge tract of ten thousand acres, which included Tom's land.

Like so many other displaced Kentucky settlers, Tom turned his attention to the millions of acres now being offered

---

[17] Cecil B. Hartley, *The Life of Daniel Boone*, 35.

across the Ohio River in the Indiana Territory. The land had first been settled in the early eighteenth century by the French, who conducted a flourishing fur trade with New Orleans by canoe and by longboat (*bateau*). Following the French and Indian War, the British gained possession of the northern territories in 1763 and ruled them for two decades, until sovereignty passed to the United States by the Treaty of Paris (1783) at the close of the Revolutionary War.

Land in Indiana was made available to prospective homesteaders by the Land Ordinance of 1785 and the Northwest Ordinance of 1787, but Indian attacks hindered settlement. The British, who continued to hold western forts in contravention of the Treaty of Paris, further encouraged Indian resistance to American sovereignty. A bitter Indian war ensued and not until Anthony Wayne's victory in 1794 over the Confederated Indian Nations at Fallen Timbers, did settlers begin to move in. Further acquisition of millions of acres of Indian land came after William Henry Harrison's victory over Tecumseh in 1811 at the Battle of Tippecanoe. Thereafter, additional tracts were obtained by artifice. A favorite ploy was to sell goods to a brave and, if he failed to pay, to hold his tribe liable. The debt, of course, would be repaid with land. Emigration began in earnest in the decade following the Indian wars. Most parties traveled down the Ohio River, which had supplanted the Wilderness Road as an entry to trans-Appalachia.

The early white inhabitants of Indiana came from Kentucky or Tennessee, drawn to the new territory by the lure of cheap land. The Ordinance of 1787 had prohibited slavery,[18] but, because of the shortage of labor, *de facto* slavery was practiced until 1810, when the loopholes were

---

[18] Slaves held in the Northwest Territory prior to 1797 were exempt from the provisions.

closed by the Territorial General Assembly. However, freed blacks were discouraged from settling in the Territory. As late as 1820, 190 slaves were still held in the southwestern corner.

By 1816, sixty thousand people had settled in Indiana, and the territory was admitted to the Union as the nineteenth state. Immediately thereafter, by Presidential Proclamation, 140,000 acres of land were offered for sale at two to three dollars per acre. Title to the land would be guaranteed by the federal government. This was the opportunity that Tom Lincoln had been waiting for.

That very year, Thomas Lincoln began preparations to leave Kentucky. Although the Knob Creek farmstead was lost to him, common law required that he be reimbursed for any improvements made on the property; but there is no evidence that he recovered money either from litigation or from quit claim. At the time, he had been married ten years, and Sarah was nine and Abraham seven. Thomas waited until after harvest before preparing to set out alone to inspect their prospective home site Indiana, less than one hundred miles away. He converted his assets into barrels of corn whiskey, an acceptable currency at the time, since it was portable and had a long shelf life. Whiskey distillation was a thriving business in nearby Rolling Fork. Only corn was distilled, which could be bought for ten cents a bushel.

A mile and a half from his farm at the mouth of Knob Creek, Tom built and launched a raft. After loading the whiskey barrels and carpenter and farm tools, he lashed the cargo down with Kentucky hemp rope and floated forty miles down the Salt River to the Ohio River.

The Ohio River is divided by the Great Falls into the Upper and the Lower Ohio. The falls are at Louisville, where the river drops twenty-six feet in two miles At high water, boats can "shoot the rapids" with the help of a pilot, through a "chute" (channel) along the Indiana side of the river. At low water, teamsters and drayage were required to transport the cargos, until a by-pass canal was opened in 1830.

Fortunate for Tom, he was spared the bother of navigating the Great Falls, since the mouth of the Salt River discharged into the Ohio River ten miles below the falls. He began his fifty-mile journey down the Ohio. One may be certain that he never would have gone alone on this reconnaissance, had he not been an experienced boatman.

Even so, he narrowly escaped disaster. While floating downriver, his raft struck a submerged tree trunk, causing it to capsize.[19] With great effort, he was able to salvage most of the whiskey and his carpenter's tools. He continued on his way, encountering on the Ohio River boatmen en route to New Orleans, as well as many emigrant families traveling on overloaded rafts. He crossed the Ohio at Thompson's Ferry near Troy, Indiana, whether by ferry or by raft is not known. After leaving his cargo with a settler, he made his way north to the Little Pigeon Creek area, some eighteen miles away. A friend living in the region may have helped him make his selection of land.

The land he chose was on a gently rising slope south of the fork of Pigeon Creek and Little Pigeon Creek. It had good topsoil and lay on the edge of heavily timbered forest, which would provide him with wood and game. Early settlers avoided bottomland because of the danger of flood, mosquito and fever; and they shunned prairie because of the difficulty plowing the deep root system, at least until the advent of the self-scouring steel plow. He marked off 160 acres, a quarter section, by making blazes and piling brush. In time, he relinquished eighty acres of his quarter section to the

---

[19] Some maintain that the raft capsized on the Salt River.

government and purchased an additional twenty acres from a neighbor; so that he eventually ended up with a freehold of one hundred acres.

Tom returned on foot to Kentucky and completed the arduous preparations for departure. He built a horse-drawn wagon (or cart) and fitted it with primitive wheels and a shelter covering. Onto it, he loaded seed, bedding, spinning wheel, primitive farm implements, pewter dishes, plates, spoons, iron pots and knives and sufficient food to carry them through the winter. Wife and daughter rode; father and son walked. They tied the cow to the wagon and drove the pigs.[20]

They departed somewhat late in the year for traveling, which they would soon regret. The family spent a night with relatives in Elizabethtown and after three or four days' travel, they arrived at the Ohio River opposite Troy, Indiana. There, for the first time, the children beheld the Ohio River.

The Great Ohio! The river was one thousand miles long from its source at the Monongahela and Allegheny Rivers to its junction with the Mississippi River, its source being four hundred feet higher than the mouth. Into the Ohio River flowed three thousand miles of navigable waterways, carrying twice as much water as the Upper Mississippi. Although it looked peaceful, the river suddenly could rise sixty feet in the autumn floods and within hours sweep away fields and settlements.

They crossed the Ohio River on a crude ferry, which took them to Troy, Indiana, a small settlement and entry point for emigration. There, Tom retrieved his carpenter and farm tools and disposed of his whiskey.[21] Thomas then brought his family north for fourteen miles on a primitive trace, which

---

[20] Some state that the family walked and loaded their possessions onto two horses.

[21] In the version that has them traveling by horseback, Tom borrowed oxen and wagon for the rest of the trip.

would later become part of the Vincennes-Troy Road. The road had just been authorized by the state legislature but work had not yet begun. The homestead lay another four miles west of the trace, separated from it by dense forest, thickets and underbrush. Before the wagon could pass, trees had to be chopped down and underbrush cleared. This was the part of the journey that Abe remembered best of all.

Once arrived at their home site, Tom set about building a lean-to, to house his family through the winter. The winter must have been harrowing, despite a continuous fire at the open end to keep them warm. When spring came, Abe was given an ax and put to work. The ax would be his familiar companion for many years to come. Abe was then eight years old, and the golden rule on the frontier was "seven years of play, seven years of work, and seven years of instruction."[22]

With ax, broad ax, and handsaw and the help of other settlers, Thomas built a cabin near a spring on his property. The work took three or four days. A usual cabin was twenty feet long and fifteen feet wide, which conformed to the length of an easily manageable tree trunk. Logs were notched together at the corners and the intervening spaces filled with moss, clay or bark. Wooden pins, driven through auger holes, were used to fix the rafters to the uppermost logs and to one another. Nails were seldom used. Later, a loft was built for additional sleeping quarters. The fireplace was made of sandstone; the floor, of packed earth, and the furniture fashioned from puncheon (slabs of wood). The outbuildings included a privy and a small shelter for the livestock. Although improvements were made later, such was the early Lincoln home in Indiana. Notwithstanding, the log cabin of that era was snugger and more comfortable

---

[22] Charles Joseph Latrobe, *The Ramble in North America*, 229.

A Cabin similar to Tom Lincoln's Little Pigeon Creek home. [Lincoln Museum, Ft. Wayne, #2052]

than nowadays can be imagined. When the snows melted, Tom and some neighbors traveled to Vincennes, sixty miles away, where they made down payments on their claims. Tom's money had been converted from his whiskey assets.

Tom could then begin the backbreaking job of clearing the land, usually no more than one to two acres a year. Never did he have more than twenty acres in cultivation, no small holding for the frontier settler, since the farm implements were primitive and the iron-tipped wooden plow required careful handling. While Tom put in a crop, Nancy began her "truck patch," sowing potatoes, beans, corn, melon and squash. In accordance with the prevailing superstitions, corn was planted by the light of the moon; potatoes by the dark of the moon, etc. Tom dug a well on the property, but the farm was never as well provided with water as had been the Kentucky farms. On rare occasion, a necessary item could be obtained from the settlement on the Ohio River, which was regularly visited by store boats laden with crockery and hardware. A bugle call heralded their arrival.[23]

The Little Pigeon Creek region was then wild country. Deer, wolves, wild turkeys, ducks and wild fowl were abundant; bear and panther roamed the land and the Carolina parakeet still flocked in great numbers. A hunter had no difficulty putting meat on the table, and meat was the most important part of their diet. Tom shot or grew what they ate, and Nancy spun or weaved what they wore.

Slowly, the population of Little Pigeon Creek grew. Within four years, twenty families were living nearby. Family and friends from Kentucky came to join them, often driven out by title disputes. Nancy's cousin, the barely literate Dennis Hanks, ten years Abe's senior, also came to live with them.

---

[23] Charles Henry Ambler, *A History of Transportation in the Ohio Valley*, 75.

Daguerreotype of Thomas Lincoln.
[Lincoln Museum, Ft. Wayne, #122.]

Then, less than two years after their arrival, tragedy struck the Lincoln household. Nancy Lincoln died of the "milk sick," leaving the burden of the household management to her twelve-year-old daughter.

"Milk sick" was caused by cows feeding on the white snakeroot plant of the white aster family, which contains the poison, tremetol. The milkweed is rarely found on pastureland but is abundant on shaded land, especially on the edge of a forest. In fact, it grew within twenty feet of Nancy Lincoln's grave. Although the Lincoln family deeply regretted that a physician could not be summoned, medical treatment would have been of little avail. Apart from comforting the patient, the physician could only purge, bleed or de-worm, set or take off a limb or prescribe useless medicines.[24]

A year later, Thomas journeyed back to Elizabethtown and returned with a new wife, Sarah ("Sally") Bush Johnson, a widow with three children. She insisted on improvements to the cabin and brought with her a dowry of many useful household items, including bureau, wardrobe, chairs, bedding and crockery. These replaced the primitive furniture and the tin and pewter ware, substantially elevating the living standards in the Lincoln household.

Close bonds soon developed within the extended family. Abraham grew to love his new mother, who encouraged his appetite for learning, even though this interest may at times have irritated his father, who had less intellectual goals for his son. From the beginning, the boy was something of a disappointment to Tom, in that he showed no interest in hunting or in carpentry. So Thomas put him to work with the ax, the plow, the hoe and the scythe. In his spare time, Abe read voraciously and during the winter months, irregularly

---

[24] But in his concern for his patient, the physician of that day was unrivaled.

Portrait of Sarah (Sally) Lincoln in later years,
taken from a daguerreotype.
[Lincoln Museum, Ft. Wayne, #4396]

attended subscription schools, where he perfected his skills in reading, writing and reckoning, up to a mastery of fifth grade proportions. Slowly, the farmstead prospered, by local standards. Tom supplemented his income with carpenter work and hired out the boys for day labor: plowing, planting, hoeing and reaping and hog butchering. As Abraham grew to height of six feet four inches, he developed great strength. His services soon commanded thirty-five cents a day, still less than a man's pay. His sister, Sarah, married, but a year and a half later died during childbirth. The agony she underwent may have left in young Lincoln an abiding fear of marriage and its subsequences.

As Abe grew, so did Indiana. A nearby hamlet called Gentryville sprang up, with a general store, a blacksmith shop and a post office. Two dozen state roads were begun in 1821; three of them connecting Little Pigeon Creek to nearby county seats. The National Road, however, was initially something of a disappointment for Indiana. It had been begun back east in 1806 and was supposed to cross Indiana and Illinois to the Mississippi River. It did, in fact, reach the Ohio River at Wheeling (now West Virginia) in 1817, opening access to the Ohio River from Maryland and Virginia; but thereafter further extension westward was mired in politics.

Most important of all transportation was the Ohio River, only four hours away by foot from Little Pigeon Creek, less by horseback. As the Little Pigeon Creek and the other farmsteads slowly began to produce a surplus of agricultural products, the river took on greater importance.

Little Pigeon Baptist Church—Abe Lincoln, sexton. [Lincoln Museum, Ft. Wayne, #654.]

Around 1826, the seventeen-year-old Abe and his cousin Dennis Hanks found work along the banks of the Ohio cutting wood for the steamboats. The job was probably seasonal. Steamboat travel slackened from July-October during low water, when only shallow-draft vessels could be sure of passage; but with the fall and spring rise, traffic revived. This employment opened up for Abe Lincoln a new and exciting world.

The youths watched the procession of boats float by and quickly learned to distinguish them. For upriver travel, *Keelboats* were by now infrequent on the Ohio and Mississippi Rivers, but were still used higher up on the tributaries, where the steamboat could not venture. *Skiffs* were rowboat-size and were moved by oars or by sculling poles. The sculling pole was an oar which rested on a y-shaped lock. As in a gondola, the boatman pushed the oar to move the boat forward.

For downriver travel, there were the ubiquitous *flatboats*. The year Abe Lincoln worked the banks of the Ohio, seven thousand flatboats of forty-ton burden were crowding the western waterways.[25] Most had a two- to four-foot gunwale, but some, like the primitive *rafts*, were completely flat. *Arks* were long flatboats, pointed fore and aft, with high vertical bulwarks. These carried large cargos.

Hoards of river men furnished the labor for the river traffic. Two thousand regularly plied the waters; the rest were occasional boatmen, who had other employment. These "half horse, half alligator" roustabouts ranged up and down the Ohio and Mississippi, working, drinking, fighting and creating mischief. A well-known character was the fictional Mike Fink, who boasted that he "kin outrun, out-hop, out-jump, throw

---

[25] Leland Johnson, *Falls City Engineers*, Chap. II, *Ohio River Navigation,* 74 in http://www.usace.army.mil/publications/misc/un22/toc.htm

down, knockdown, drag out, and lick any man in the country."[26] The upriver man had herculean strength, demanded by his employment. Keelboat men and bargemen were natural enemies of the flatboat men, and the fighting was often violent.[27] As time wore on, the patience of the public for the antics of the river men notably waned.

Most exciting of all the river craft were the steamboats. They had been conceived by John Fitch in 1786, although other contemporaries also had contributed. In 1807, the well-trained engineer, Robert Fulton, built the *Clermont*, using an English engine and an American hull. In 1811, Nicholas Roosevelt captained the first steamboat on the western waters. While underway, the *New Orleans* encountered the terrible New Madrid Earthquake, but was able to continue on to New Orleans. However, its engine lacked the power for the return upriver. Four years later, the *Enterprise*, with a high-pressure engine, made two round trips between New Orleans and Louisville. It took the *Washington* forty-one days in 1816 to make a round trip from Louisville to New Orleans. By 1822, the trip could be made downriver from Troy to New Orleans in seven days and the return in sixteen days. Within a decade, 150 steamboats were plying the western river ways. Sidewheelers were more popular than sternwheelers, provided that a sufficiently wide navigation channel was assured.[28]

The young Lincoln watched the crowded procession of river craft, loaded with poultry, pork, cornmeal, flour, whiskey, venison, nuts, skins, furs and ginseng. He visited the "floating stores," and inspected their wares of furniture, kitchenware, plows, clothes, notions, wagons and harness. Barter was extensively used, since hard currency was scarce.

---

[26] Ambler, *A History of Transportation*, 57.
[27] Ibid., 51.
[28] Riegel, *America Moves West,* 222.

The silver pieces in circulation were divided into "bits," eight to the dollar, each of which could be detached to make change. Banknotes ("shinplasters") were regarded with suspicion. They were issued by distant banks[29] and accepted only at a discount.

Life ashore and afloat was governed by the hazards of the river. Annual floods shifted sand and gravel bars, created and destroyed islands, swept trees and cut new channels. Obstructions, sunken rocks and fallen trees were a constant threat to navigation. That very year (1827), nineteen steamboats and innumerable flatboats were lost, chiefly after colliding with obstacles.[30]

Not until 1828, did Congress vote $30,000 to remove obstacles on the Ohio River, the first of twelve annual appropriations. The work was delegated to the Corps of Engineers or to their subcontractors. Both political parties supported the Ohio River improvements. Even Andrew Jackson, the quintessential "States' Rights" man, gave his support, although he opposed other internal improvements, at the cost of seeing the rival Whig Party gain in popularity in his own home state of Tennessee.

Troy was well known to the river traffic. The village gained notoriety in 1825 during Lafayette's triumphant return tour of the United States, when his steamboat went aground and sunk near the town. Fortunately, no lives were lost. Troy had a hardwood lumberyard, which supplied the steamboats. Wood sold for two dollars a cord,[31] and steamboats consumed one cord an hour.[32] When the steamboat sounded its whistle

---

[29] Sandburg, *The Prairie Years*, 48.
[30] Davidson, *The Rivers of America,* Vol. 1, 240.
[31] One cord equals 128 square feet.
[32] W. Bullock, *Sketch of a Journey through the Eastern States*, Microfilm XBB-110 NYPL.

mid-river, skiffs scurried to bring it wood. At other times, the steamboat would tie up at the landing. While the wood was being on-loaded, passengers could disembark to stretch their legs and chat with the people on shore.

Abe later found work as a part-time ferryman at Bates' Landing, a mile from Troy. He ferried passengers to the steamboats waiting in the channel. In his spare time, he built his own flat-bottomed skiff and used it to scull passengers. The law prohibited him from transporting travelers across the river to the Kentucky side, but not to a steamboat waiting mid-river. It was while sculling two passengers out to a steamboat, that Lincoln earned his first dollar, the equivalent of three days' pay.

Sometime in 1828, James Gentry, a merchant, arranged to send a flatboat on a 1,400-mile trip to New Orleans. He had made the trip before and on one occasion had taken his son, Allen, with him. This time, he would send Allen and another hand.

Abe Lincoln was offered a job as "bow hand," at a salary of eight dollars a month and "found." Lincoln was chosen for his size, strength, and for his willingness to accept less than the regular wage of a riverboat man. He had heard his father tell about his trip (or trips?) to New Orleans and had listened attentively to the stories of the river men, so that he had some knowledge of the customs and challenges of the river.

Lincoln helped with the construction of the flatboat. It was built along the banks of Pigeon Creek near Rockport, fifteen miles west of Troy, where Alan Gentry lived. Rockport itself was situated on a hundred-foot bluff. Large stone columns nearby gave the town its early name of "Hanging Rock." In his father's day, it had been the haunt of river pirates, who were thought to have hidden their loot in a nearby cave.

Lincoln, the skiff owner. [Lincoln Museum, Ft. Wayne, #321]

The measurements of the rectangular flatboat are not known. Some flatboats could be as long as one hundred feet; but these required a larger crew.

The only tools[33] used by the two boatwrights were the crosscut saw, a mill saw, an axe, a broadaxe, an auger and a drawknife. Iron nails were not used in the construction. The gunwales were made from two flat pieces of poplar log thirty to fifty feet in length, two to three feet in breadth and a foot in thickness. Into the gunwales were mortised crosspieces of oak, fourteen feet long, six inches wide and three inches thick, in addition to six-inch head blocks at each end. Onto the crosspiece frame, two-inch longitudinal oak planks were fastened by means of one-inch-square oak pins, which were driven through an auger hole through both planks by a heavy maul. A bottom, made of two-inch longitudinal planks, was then attached to the longitudinal planks and rabbeted onto the gunwales. Oakum and pitch were then spread to watertight the bottom.

The boat was turned over and launched with the aid of windlass and lever. To build up the hull, uprights were mortised into the upper edge of the gunwales and onto them, one-and-a-half-inch poplar planks were attached longitudinally; and the seams caulked and pitched with oakum. A false bottom was often constructed, since the raft was not entirely watertight.

With a complement of only two men, Gentry's boat was something like forty feet long, eighteen feet wide, with two-foot poplar gunwales and a two-inch plank bottom.[34] In the stern, it would have a "streamer" (rudder), a board attached to a long pole to steer the boat in the current. This, Gentry would

---

[33] Henry C. Whitney, "Lincoln the Citizen," in *Life and Works of Abraham Lincoln*. Rahway: Quinn and Boden, 1909, p. 49.
[34] Davidson, *The Rivers of America,* Vol. 1, 201.

man. In the bow, Lincoln would man the "gouger," a small oar to help steer the boat in unusually rapid water. In addition, the boat might have two oars ("sweeps" or "broadhorns"), to steady the craft and help move it to shore. There would be a check-post in the bow for purchase, when the boat had to be pulled off a sandbar or a shallow. A line ("houser") would be fixed to the check-post, then wrapped around a nearby tree and pulled by as many hands as could be summoned, or by a team of oxen.[35]

Food was cooked on a crude firebox made of flat stone; or on shore. A small deck house provided shelter from inclement weather. Some flatboats had a shed for animals. Often, a small canoe was brought along, so that the crew could go ashore, without the bother of landing the flatboat. Apparently, the Gentry flatboat did not have a canoe. Some flatboats were flimsily built ("packing cases"), but most were made with care commensurate with the skill of the builder and the worth of the cargo. Small flatboats do not necessarily mean safer flatboats, especially if the craft were overloaded. Accidents and disasters were a daily occurrence among boatmen.

Work on the flatboat began in October 1828, after harvest. Construction of the hull was done bottom side up at the water's edge. When the hull was completed, the craft was righted by fastening one end of a rope around the gunwales to the bottom of the flatboat and winding the other end over a tree limb, before fastening it to a team of oxen or reeving it through a block and tackle. Once righted, the flatboat was launched on rollers. The shelter or shed was constructed when the craft was afloat.

---

[35] Riegel, *America Moves West,* 220.

Lincoln as flatboat man.
[Lincoln Museum, Ft. Wayne, #323.]

A spectator present at the launching would have seen in the nineteen-year-old Lincoln a tall, tough, wiry youth, dressed in buckskin breeches, linsey-woolsey shirt and coonskin cap, hard at work loading the barrels of corn, pork, and bacon. Great care was taken to evenly distribute the barrels and to lash them down securely, so that they would not shift and upset the boat. Doubtless, Abe recalled his father's misadventure.

Departure was delayed until Allen Gentry's wife had given birth to their son in December. The departure of a flatboat could be the occasion for a well-attended party,[36] but it is unlikely there was much celebration for these two youths. Lincoln may have returned home to bid goodbye to his family and to receive last-minute advice from his father, who had made the trip two decades before.

At last, the journey was underway, with Abe at the sweeps, Allen at the streamer. It would be a grievous error to suppose the two had merely to sit back and let the flatboat take itself downriver to New Orleans. Every minute afloat required great vigilance; every mile presented dangers. Where the current was slow, the rudders had little effect on steerage. There were few straight channels. Sandbars and islands could suddenly appear, and the crew had to exercise critical judgment in choosing the correct channel or "chute," in order to avoid the obstacle.

A few pilot manuals were available to help the boatman; among them the popular *Cummings Western Pilot*,[37] but the information was not always reliable, since the rivers could, and did, change courses between editions. Even if the boatman had the book, he could not completely rely on this otherwise valuable help. A steamboat pilot or a well-to-do boatman

---

[36] Ambler, *A History of Transportation,* 50.
[37] Samuel Cummings, *The Western Pilot*, 1834.

might own a current copy; the less affluent, an older edition; and the poor flatboat man might now and again have an opportunity to peek at someone else's book. There were enough around, so that a boatman might even be able to copy one of its many maps. More commonly, the flatboat man relied on the advice of other river men and people on shore. Even seemingly helpful information could not always be trusted. Landsmen sometimes profited when a flatboat foundered.

The Cummings guide instructed the boatman:

> "Two miles below Rockport is a bar on the right: channel pretty near to the left shore, until nearly up with Puppy Creek on the left, then keep well over to the right shore above Yellow Bank Islands, and when within half a mile on the first, (a small island pretty close to the right shore) steer pretty short over to the left shore: opposite the head of the second, or large island, is a sunken ledge of rocks, about 50 yards from the left shore; incline a little to the right past them, and then toward the left shore again..."[38]

Once underway, the crew was ready to pole off snags, ease the flatboat into the proper channel, or, when caught in a tangle of driftwood, to quickly ax their craft free. Otherwise, the flatboat might drift under the obstruction and capsize when the cargo shifted.

Each obstacle had its own name. *Sawyers* were trees fixed to the river bottom which came to the surface; *sleeping sawyers* were trees that float below the surface; *snags* and *planters* projected a foot or less above the surface; and *rafts* (*wooden islands*) were floating mats of trees.[39]

---

[38] Cummings, *The Western Pilot* (1829), 42.
[39] Ambler, *A History of Transportation,* 47.

The two youths drank from the river and emptied their wastes into it. They fished for pike, catfish and perch and sold their surplus to the smokehouses on shore or to the other boatmen. Like all their fellow boatmen, they were ready to spring to the assistance of another boat in distress. They traveled during the daylight hours and tied up at dusk to search for firewood and prepare their meal.

The flatboat crept along at a speed of one to three miles an hour. Although the Ohio River was often a half-mile wide, the navigable channels could be no wider than a few rods.[40] They passed extensive groves of cottonwood and thick, impenetrable cane-brakes, some twenty feet high, in which an occasional bear was seen.[41] Dense forests ran inland. Rocky ledges and cragged spurs reached out to the water's edge. Great slices of the clay banks fell into the river, giving it a dull gold color.

Between bluffs and river was a small strip of land called "bottom," whose alluvium had an unrivalled fertility. The Lower Ohio was slowly becoming a great corn (Indiana) and tobacco producer (Kentucky). They saw the tops of Indian corn and the fences, roofs and chimneys of small settlements, built atop the wooded bluffs, to escape the yearly inundations.[42] When constructed on bottom land, the cabins were often erected on pilings.

---

[40] A rod equals 5 ½ yards.
[41] Hall, *Letters from the West*, 188.
[42] Latrobe, *A Ramble in North America,* 111.

A passing flatboat.
[Lincoln Museum, Ft. Wayne, #3424.]

They passed the expected landmarks: Little Hurricane Island, French Islands, the beautiful Three Mile Island and, on the Indiana side, Evansville. They saw Hendersonville on the Kentucky side, where the famous birdman Audubon had lived for a few years. Neighbors were mystified by the strange man, whose hair dangled down to his shoulders. Diamond Island, Straight Island, Slim Island went by. Huge sycamores grew in perfusion on both sides of the river, some with a trunk circumference of thirty to fifty feet.

Flocks of swallows screamed and circled the boat. Sandpipers bobbed their little tails; redbirds trilled; blue herons waded daintily in sandy shallows and turkey buzzards rose and wheeled about in midair.[43] Floating stores drew up

---

[43] R.G. Thwaites, *Afloat on the Ohio*, 262.

alongside them, containing tin shops and blacksmith and liquor shops.

Pirate boats pushing off from shore were always a threat, much less so than in Tom Lincoln's day. Steamboats swept by, rocking the flatboat in its wake. Some steamboat pilots enjoyed smashing the sweeps. A few passengers waved, others greeted them with derision, some, on request, threw them their old newspapers.

The mouth of the clear, swift Wabash River was passed, its bluffs crowned with walnut and pecan groves. The Wabash and its tributaries were the most important (but not the largest) effluents of the Ohio River, draining a wonderfully fertile countryside.[44] Steamboats could ascend the Wabash all the way to Vincennes and Terre Haute. In 1826, the river carried 152 flatboats, laden with 250,000 bushels of corn, 100,000 barrels of pork, 2,500 cattle and five tons of beeswax.[45] The river formed the boundary between Indiana and Illinois, but its course varied with the rainfall.

They floated by Wabash Island, covered with woodland, and Brown Island. Four miles below Brown Island, 150 miles into their journey, they came to Shawneetown, Illinois.

Shawneetown, the storied dwelling place of Tecumseh, was worth a boatman's visit. It was here that emigrants bound for Illinois and Missouri debarked. Fine farms extended down the slope to the water's edge. Built atop a bluff, Shawneetown now had one hundred houses, some of brick, as well as shops and taverns. It was "gradually becoming the commercial emporium of southern Illinois."[46] The disenchanted called it "ague town," because of the frequent occurrence of marsh fever and dumb ague.

---

[44] Cummings *The Western Pilot* (1829), 44.
[45] Walter McDougall, *Freedom just around the Corner*, 433.
[46] Edmund Flagg, *The Far West,* Vol. 2, 35

Twenty miles below Shawneetown, they came to Hurricane Island which, on the Illinois side, faced Cave-in-Rock. The cave was guarded by black jagged rocks which formed a semi-elliptical arch forty feet high and eighty feet wide.[47] In the back of the cave was a passage leading up to an upper room, where the skeletons of sixty men were found, said to be the remains of murdered boatmen. As many as thirty robbers camped at nearby Hurricane Island and lured the boatmen to their doom. The pirates were finally disbursed by the Kentucky militia, but some found their way to the Mississippi Territory, where they continued their murderous practices. The cave was subsequently used as a place of public entertainment. A sign posted in front advertised: "Wilson's Liquor Vault and House of Entertainment."

Steamboats encountered a dangerous shoal at the Cave-in-Rock, sometimes forcing them to unload and kedge, to free themselves.[48] The instructions of Cummings were implicit: "Keep near the right shore for about 4 miles below Shawneetown, then cross short over to the left shore…"[49]

Several wooded islands were approached, which required careful maneuvering. Embankments formed by the overflowing river sometimes left natural levees eight to ten feet high. On the Kentucky side, they passed the mouth of the Cumberland River, which, in ordinary good stages of water, was navigable for steamboats as far up as Nashville; and for flat and keelboats, to a much greater distance.[50] At the mouth of the Cumberland River, was the little village of Galcona, Kentucky, once a rendezvous of Aaron Burr. The mouth was a frequent stop for steamboats, since a cord of wood was fifty

---

[47] Ibid., 36.
[48] Latrobe, *A Ramble in North America,* 114.
[49] Cummings, *The Western Pilot* (1829), 44.
[50] Ibid., 45.

cents cheaper than elsewhere. Two months after the Gentry flatboat floated by, Andrew Jackson would come down the Cumberland and proceed by steamboat up the Ohio River to Pittsburgh, on his way to Washington to take Presidential office.

A few islands later, they reached the mouth of the Tennessee River, the largest tributary of the Ohio River, navigable for large boats for more than six hundred miles. At the mouth were a few scattered houses, which would later become Paducah, Kentucky, named for a captive Indian woman sacrificed by a band of Pawnee. Eight miles below the mouth, some boatman might have pointed out the ruins of Fort Massac on the Illinois side, where the French garrison was massacred by the Indians in the French and Indian War. Local settlers were fond of recounting the story. As they floated by the monotonous clay banks, they passed several small settlements of what would later acquire familiar names.

Steamboat passengers complained that the lower portion of the Ohio was quite devoid of beauty.[51] Bluffs began to disappear and cultivation became less frequent, replaced by swamp and inland forest.[52] Pilings for the bottomland houses were often seen.

Soon they approached the perilous "Grand Chain," a two-mile stretch of rocks, extending up to four miles from the Mississippi junction. These rocks had caused more wrecks than any other part of the river. In the early days, special pilots were required to guide the steamboats through the chain. Robbers ("boat wreckers") were known to pose as pilots and deliberately pile the boat onto the rocks. Congress had

---

[51] "Rubio" [James Thomas Horton], *Rambles in the United States and Canada*, 121.
[52] Timothy Flint, *Recollections of the last Ten Years*, 84.

recently authorized the removal of some of these rocks, as well as other improvements, but work had not yet begun.

At the junction of the Ohio and the Mississippi Rivers stood a small settlement. Cummings instructed the boatman: "There is a good landing above the Mouth of the Ohio; if you do not wish to land, keep pretty well by the left from half a mile above the mouth to clear the bar on the right below the point."[53]

For the first time, Lincoln cast his eyes on the mighty Mississippi River. He had read something of its early exploration in William Grimshaw's *History of the United States*. Hernando De Soto, with six hundred armor-breasted men, was the first European to cast eyes on the Mississippi River. His party crossed the river in 1542, below its junction with the Arkansas River. More than a century passed before the Europeans showed further interest in the Mississippi. Then, from a mistaken belief that the river might flow into the Gulf of California and thus provide a shortcut for travel to the Pacific, interest rekindled. The Marquette-Joliet expedition of 1673 traced the course of the Mississippi to its junction with the Arkansas River (where De Soto had crossed). In 1682, La Salle voyaged down the Illinois River to the Mississippi, then, in a later expedition, paddled by canoe the full length of the Mississippi to the Gulf of Mexico, where he proclaimed the sovereignty of Louis XIV and heralded French domination of the Mississippi Valley.

As the flatboat glided onto the Mississippi, the river took on a different appearance. Travelers noted that instead of the sweet, pretty Ohio, it became a grand, majestic brute. It lost its friendliness and was now to be feared.[54] Abruptly, the waters

---

[53] Ibid., 49.
[54] Willard Price, *The Amazing Mississippi*, 112, 114.

become turbid. An "ocean of pea soup," wrote one traveler.[55] "A slimy monster," wrote Dickens, "An enormous ditch… running liquid mud…its strong and frothy current choked and obstructed everywhere by huge logs and whole forest trees."[56] To Mark Twain it was "the majestic, magnificent Mississippi …shining in the sun."[57]

The lower Mississippi had a median width of one mile but during the spring rise, the river could become fifty miles wide. It moved four to six miles per hour, regularly eroding its banks. Changes of weather were frequent and wrought havoc with the river traffic. At the first sign of an approaching storm, the crew had to turn the clumsy and lumbering flatboat toward a sheltered shore. Wrecks were a constant reminder of delay and misjudgment.

The west bank of the lower Mississippi was a broad flood plain, twenty-five to 125 miles in width, punctuated with oxbow lakes and marshes, remaining from the former channels. On the east bank was a succession of twelve high bluffs. The channel seemed to favor the eastern bank, leaving swampland to the west. For much of its length, there were natural levees bordering the river, built up from sediment that had been carried and deposited in times of flood.

Unlike the rivers of the Atlantic coast, the Mississippi has innumerable bends. These are semi-circular turns, often more than twenty miles in circuit, bordered by many bayous, choked with floating trees and aquatic plants. In one instance, a thirty-mile bend came within one mile of completing the circle. The deepest channels were often in the bend, with the strongest current at the concavity, and the heaviest shoals directly

---

[55] "Rubio," 143.
[56] Charles Dickens, *American Waters*, 126.
[57] Mark Twain [Samuel Clemens], *Life on the Mississippi*, 26.

opposite.[58] Because of its serpentine course, the boatman could see only few miles ahead. Suddenly, a steamboat might loom before them, and their fate would depend on the skill and concern of the pilot. Boatmen calculated distance not by miles but by bends. Often, they had to travel five miles to gain one mile, as the crow flies.

As they floated downriver, sounds of the fiddle wafted from passing flatboats. The youths fished for catfish, which they sold to nearby plantations. Sails would have been of no use to them, since the prevailing wind was in the opposite direction.[59]

Often, the crews lashed their boats together, while they exchanged gossip and talked politics. Andrew Jackson, the hero of the day and the idol of the common man, had just been elected to the Presidency a month before. There was speculation that he would expel the Cherokee, Choctaw and the Chickasaw Nations from their lands in Tennessee, Mississippi and elsewhere; and make the region available for settlement.

Twenty-five miles south of the mouth of the Ohio, just within the southern border of Missouri, they passed New Madrid on a great bend of the river. The town had a special fascination for the boatmen, for it was here that the Great Earthquake of 1811 struck, which destroyed the town, killed hundreds of people and dammed up the Mississippi River so that, for a few hours, it flowed backwards (i.e., north). The tremors were felt as far away as Boston and New Orleans and were followed by two thousand aftershocks, recurring into the next year. Now, the town was merely a wood stop for the steamboats. Wolf Island glided by, twenty-five miles in circumference, which had only one inhabitant.

---

[58] A. Parker, *Trip to the West and Texas*, 229.
[59] Price, *The Amazing Mississippi,* 52, 53.

On the west side, the Arkansas Territory began. A thin band of settlement lay along the banks, which could be visited whenever the channel took them over to the less inviting Arkansas side.

On the eastern shore, settlement in Tennessee had already penetrated a hundred miles into Chickasaw territory. Whites had settled among the Chickasaw, married their women, and helped the Nation become successful traders. The Chickasaws conducted trade with the Mississippi traffic and with travelers journeying along the Natchez Trace. The Chickasaw were not roaming bands of savages, but native people who had mastered the ways of the white man and learned to profit from them. They lived in eight hundred houses, a few worth one thousand dollars or more. Most had sheds for cattle; some had barns.

Andrew Jackson saw great possibilities in this region. After his victory in New Orleans, Jackson led troops up the Natchez Trace and in 1816 compelled a treaty with the Chickasaw at Doak's Stand, forcing the Nation to cede land. His business partners helped found a trading settlement, which later became Memphis. Now that Jackson had been elected to the Presidency, further cessions from the Nations were expected. Many of the Choctaw had already moved across the river to the Arkansas Territory, to disassociate themselves from the avaricious white men.

They passed a series of four bluffs above the eastern shore. At the summit of the fourth, lay a small settlement called Memphis (Fourth Chickasaw Bluffs), still in Chickasaw territory. The landing may have detained them briefly, but the town was then hardly worth a visit.

The delta began at Memphis and extended all the way to the Gulf of Mexico. For the first time, Abe saw cotton fields and learned about their cultivation. Like corn, the cotton plant is grown annually from seed. The pods grow to the size of a walnut and, when ripe, open in quarters. Picking commenced in September; one acre yielding seven hundred pounds of cotton.[60] The slave used thumb and finger to pick the cotton ball. Each slave was expected to "make" seven bales a year.[61] After the picking, the cotton ball was ginned to separate the seed, which in turn was compressed to yield one gallon of oil for each one hundred pounds of seed.[62] The cotton was then put up in bales for shipment downriver.

Flatboat men used every opportunity to sell their cargo to the small farmer and plantation managers. Where the plantation owner himself made the purchase, flatboat men might have to bribe the manager before they could approach the owner.[63] The plantation purchased one barrel of second or third quality beef or pork per annum for each slave.[64] Pork, beef, corn, cornmeal, flour, and potatoes were sold off and sometimes bartered for cotton, or, further down the Mississippi, for sugar.

The state of Mississippi bordered the Mississippi River for four hundred miles. The area was wet, low, hot and unhealthy, overrun with mosquito swamps, hardwood trees and thick tangles of impenetrable canebrakes. Most challenging of all was the Yazoo delta, with its seven thousand square miles of floodplain. In some areas, sediment had been deposited on the riverbed, so that the surface of the river lay above the bordering shore. Withal, the Yazoo delta was incredibly fertile. A few settlers had trickled in after the Revolutionary War, but now, more were pouring in, in

---

[60] Cummins, *The Western Pilot* (1834), 90.
[61] Parker, *A Trip to the West and Texas,* 157.
[62] James Stuart, *Three Years in North America*, 90.
[63] Price, *The Amazing Mississippi*, 53.
[64] J.M. Peck, *New Guide for Emigrants to the West*, 113.

anticipation of Choctaw displacement. As elsewhere, the high mortality from flood and mosquito favored larger holdings, where white overseers supervised slave labor.

South of the mouth of the Yazoo, they saw a settlement atop a high bluff and a landing crowded with many flatboats. The pilot book described Vicksburg as a large village, with a number of "stores, lawyers and physicians, etc."[65] It had once been a Choctaw trading site, before it passed through a succession of Spanish and British rules, before finally coming into American hands. Many of its plantation owners lived elsewhere and left the supervision of their estate to a manager.[66]

The boys sold produce at the farms and plantations along both banks of the river. On one occasion, Allen Gentry was paid with counterfeit bills, which he promptly passed on to another victim. Lincoln assured Allen that his father would not reproach him for doing this.[67]

They floated downriver to Natchez, a town of three thousand people, situated three hundred feet above the river. Cummings directed the boatman: "As you approach the right hand point above Natchez, incline toward the left shore, to avoid the large bar on the right, above the town."[68] Overhead, they saw white-headed eagles, fishing hawks, orchard orioles and flycatchers.

The city had early been populated with New England colonists and Acadian farmers, before passing through the familiar succession of British, French and Spanish sovereignties.

---

[65] Cummings, *The Western Pilot* (1829), 64.
[66] Jonathan Daniels, *The Devil's Backbone*, 242.
[67] Ward H. Lamon, *The Life of Abraham Lincoln*, 71.
[68] Cummings, *The Western Pilot* (1829), 71.

Natchez was divided into two towns, one atop, the other below the bluff. The notorious Natchez-under-the-Hill had a mile-long landing, reeking of garbage, river muck and the smell of raw whiskey. Some called it the "most profligate place in the country," referring to its five houses of prostitution, one of them on a floating flatboat. Black, white and octoroon prostitutes hung half-naked out of hovels, seeking to lure the flatboat man. The boatmen crowding the streets were, as the quite imaginative Mark Twain described them:

> "a rough and hardy men; rude, uneducated, brave, suffering terrific hardships with sailor-like stoicism; heavy drinkers, coarse frolickers...heavy fighters, reckless fellows everyone, elephantinely jolly, foul-witted, profane, prodigal of their money, bankrupt at the end of the trip, fond of barbaric finery, prodigious braggarts, yet, in the main, honest, trustworthy, faithful to promises and duty, and often picturesquely magnanimous."[69]

In this environment, the two youths would have been hard pressed to defend their cargo, so it is not likely that they tarried long in that town, apart from taking turns at going ashore for a few minutes so that they could later brag that they had been there. Both were sure to be closely questioned upon their return home about their visit to that den of inequity.

After Natchez, not a hill was to be seen during the rest of their trip. Cypress forests, covered with Spanish moss, now gave the woods a malignant appearance. Marsh fumes stirred fearsome worries.

Several islands crept by. Eighty miles below Natchez, they came to a long bend or "bow," into which the Red River discharged, after having passed three hundred miles through

---

[69] Mark Twain [Samuel Clemens]. *Life on the Mississippi,* 11.

Louisiana. The Red River had a dark red color and was even more turbid than the Mississippi. As it approached its junction with the Mississippi, it broke up into a maze of islands and lakes, reminding some of the Nile delta. One huge five-hundred-square-mile floating island, called the "Great Raft," was composed of trapped timber. Because of the obstructions, travel along this almost circular bend of the Mississippi was especially hazardous.[70]

Six miles below the mouth of the Red River they saw the first of three bayous of the Mississippi. The first, the "Atchafalaya," was an ancient bed of the Red River. It flowed four hundred miles to the Gulf and carried from the Mississippi as much water as the Red River brought to it.

Below the Red River, sugar plantations began to appear. They had now come to the "sugar coast." Before 1795, sugar was grown chiefly to make rum, but then a method of granulating sugar was introduced, which greatly stimulated cultivation. Sugar cost more to grow than cotton, but was three times more profitable.[71] Rice, at the time, was least rewarding. It was called "Providence Rice," since exacting conditions for cultivation were required. Rice was introduced by the priests in 1718, but the crop was not grown in large quantity until a half century after Lincoln's visit.

Eighty miles below Natchez, they came to Baton Rouge and saw the first rising ground since Natchez, albeit only thirty to forty-nine feet above the high water mark. Baton Rouge then had only twelve hundred people. Set back from the levees were the sugar plantations, and handsome, fresh-painted houses, surrounded by magnolias.

The two drifted six miles past Baton Rouge and tied up for the night near the plantation of a Creole woman, a

---

[70] Latrobe, *The Ramble in North America,* 279.
[71] "Rubio," *Rambles in the United States*, 148.

Madame Duchesne, at whose estate they hoped to transact business in the morning. During the night, seven renegade slaves began boarding the flatboat, intent on murdering the youths and stealing the cargo. Gentry tried to bluff them by calling to Lincoln: "Bring the guns! Shoot them!" Lincoln grabbed a club and managed to beat them off. They gave chase, but the marauders escaped. Returning to the boat, they hastily cut loose and floated a few miles down river, to wait for dawn. Lincoln received a cut in the melee, which left a small scar, but whether on neck or forehead is disputed.

After Baton Rouge, the river widened to the breadth of a mile and had fewer obstacles and obstructions. Settlements became more frequent. Plantation seemed to adjoin plantation, extending a mile back into cypress forests. Some had noble homes and steam-powered mills.

They traveled one hundred miles downriver until finally, on a great bend in the river, they looked down and saw an enormous city of forty thousand people. New Orleans was situated ten feet below sea level on something of an island, surrounded by the Mississippi River, three lakes and another river. Across from it were the shipyards.

A forest of masts and stacks stretched along the levee.[72] On a typical day, twenty steamboats might be in port, along with sixty large ship-rigged vessels and 125 schooners, brigs and sloops, all broadside to the levee, two to three deep. Further downriver, hundreds of flatboats and keelboats were tied up for two to three miles, some lashed five abreast.[73] Sailors, planters, venders, boatmen, hawkers, all crowded the levee street, speaking in a myriad of languages. Instead of wharfs and piers, there were large wooden platforms,[74] piled

---

[72] Stuart, *Three Years in North America,* 197.

[73] Latrobe, *The Ramble in North America,* Vol. 2, 332.

[74] Stuart, *Three Years in North America,* 197.

high with bales of cotton and hogsheads of sugar and tobacco. Gangs of black stevedores scrambled to load the wares onto drays, carts and wagons, which carried the produce to bustling warehouses, where they awaited transshipment to Europe or the eastern cities of the United States. Idle river men congregated along a stretch known as the "swamp," where they talked, fought, played and sought their own kind of refreshment and entertainment.

On the levee, New Orleans.
[Lincoln Museum, Ft. Wayne, #4638.]

Gentry sold the cargo at a profit, and then he sold the flatboat, which usually fetched eight to twelve dollars. The youths had only a few days to see the sights. City life was animated during January. The inhabitants had long since returned from the yellow fever exodus, which had begun in August. The climate was now adjudged to be healthy, and people were in high spirits.

The old city, where the French-speaking people lived, was built in the shape of a parallelogram. With its narrow, cobblestone streets and drainage gutters, it resembled an old French provincial town. The two marveled at the houses with their facings of white or yellow stucco, the balconies, the projecting roofs and the iron grillwork. The English-speaking population occupied the suburbs, called *fauxbourgs*. Here, houses were built of brick and had an "American" design.

Adjacent to the levee was the market, which sprang to life at sunrise and was filled by 7:00 am. Peddlers and merchants spoke French, but an interpreter could be found for a likely customer. Doubtless, the two bought small gifts for their families, such as combs, mirrors and sheathed knives. The grand, whitewashed Catholic cathedral and the small Presbyterian Church were both worthy of inspection. Also, the city had both a French and an English theater, but it is unlikely the two attended, since the price of admission was two dollars.[75] Women of doubtful character were seldom seen on the streets, men were on hand to advise the stranger where they could be found.[76]

A third of the population was black; a few of them freemen, well dressed and with proud bearings. Chained slaves cleaned the streets. Dozens of other slaves were driven by whips across the plaza. Broadsides advertised the daily slave sales: "Several likely girls from 12 to 18 years old"; "Forty-five negroes now on hand." Admission to the slave auctions was free. Some spectators attended for prurient amusement. Hundreds of slaves were sold during the few days the youths were in the city, to satisfy the ever-growing needs of the canebrakes, rice swamps and the cotton fields.[77] Such

---

[75] Ibid., 199.
[76] Ibid., 201.
[77] Ibid., 207.

were the horrifying sights witnessed by the nineteen-year-old, a youth whose humanitarian sensibilities kept him from shooting game, killing a turtle, or mistreating an animal. The memory of these inhumanities remained with him for the rest of his life.

After a stay of only two or three days in New Orleans, they took passage on a steamboat bound for St. Louis. For the poor, backwoods youth, his first steamboat trip was another memorable experience.

At the time, the steamboat had an average length of two hundred feet; and had two decks and a roof. On the lower (main) deck were the fireboxes for the four to eight boilers, placed mid-ship for the sidewheelers between the paddle wheel boxes, and towards the stern, for the sternwheelers.[78] Cargo was stored on the lower (main) deck on every inch of space that could be found. The second deck, which extended from stern almost to the bow, housed the regular (cabin) passengers. It had staterooms to accommodate twenty or more travelers, dining room, galley, men's smoking room, ladies parlor and library.[79] Above the second deck was the roof, also called the third deck, where the pilothouse was situated. Deck passengers were assigned to the roof and were not permitted on the cabin deck. They brought their own bedding and provisions and did their own cooking on stoves proved by the steamboat.

The deck passenger paid seven dollars for the trip from New Orleans to St. Louis, but two dollars was remitted, if he agreed to help with the wood loading, and some other duties.[80] Cabin passengers paid twenty-five dollars.[81] The steamboat

---

[78] Latrobe, *The Ramble in North America,* Vol.1, 284.
[79] Riegel, *America Moves West,* 223.
[80] Ibid., 223.
[81] Parker,*A Trip to the West and Texas,* 115.

stopped at least twice daily to renew its supply of wood. The deck passengers would be summoned with the call: "Wood-pile! Wood-pile! Where are the wooders!"[82] Often, only half the deck passengers responded, while the rest hid out. In addition to loading the firewood, deck passengers were expected to help the slaves feed wood into the fireboxes, clean the decks and attend to the animals. One traveler noted that the deck passenger was often treated like a dog.[83]

The boat carried a captain, mate, two engineers, two pilots, a clerk, two or three stewards and perhaps ten hired deck slaves.[84] The pilot was paid $125 a month and was virtually in command once the steamboat was underway. His was a job to which every boy aspired. At the time of boarding, spirits was often made available to all the passengers and also to the crew, including the deck slaves.[85]

Steamboat travel entailed risk. In the first four decades of steamboat travel, four thousand casualties resulted from steamboat accidents. The bottom of a boat could rip open on a snag and sink in few minutes.[86] Chimney embers could cause devastating fires on these wooden vessels, and spread to the readily flammable cotton cargo. The boiler might burst, especially if the engineer were drunk or otherwise inattentive to mounting pressure. Some engineers were no more than jumped-up firemen.[87] Charles Dickens always insisted on a stateroom away from the boilers: "The wonder is, not that there should be so many fatal accidents, but that any journey shall be safely made."[88] Steamboats with high-pressure

[82] Ibid., 116.
[83] Price, *The Amazing Mississippi,* 58.
[84] Stuart, *Three Years in North America,* 241.
[85] Ibid., 246.
[86] Riegel, *America Moves West,* 223.
[87] "Rubio,"*Rambles in the United States,* 152.
[88] Dickens, *American Notes,* 143.

engines were preferred, since mud could be blown out of the safety valve, thus reducing the danger of an accumulation in the boiler.[89] On a trip to St. Louis, at least two boiler stops were required. Captains often took in tow, sometimes for long distances, another steamboat or several heavily laden barges.[90]

The trip to St. Louis took a week. As they approached the town, passengers noted that the navigable channel veered toward the Illinois side. Shoals were being deposited along the St. Louis waterfront, threatening to leave the city inland.[91] Years later, Lt. Robert E. Lee would come to the town's rescue, by constructing jetties and levees.

At the time of Lincoln's visit, St. Louis was still a center for the fur trade and a shipping port for nearby lead mines.[92] Not for another decade would it become the *entrepot* for the western migration.

Their stay in town was brief. Many found St. Louis to be unhealthy, its murky atmosphere loaded with the miasmas of a thousand swamps. Grog shops were scattered along the wharfs, and a few coffee houses beckoned, with their billiard tables.[93] The town was built on a slight rise. Its three crooked and narrow streets were somewhat randomly laid out, which gave the town a comfortable feeling. Many buildings had tumble-down galleries (balconies), approachable by stairs or by a ladder.[94] Every home seemed to have a stoop.[95]

Visitors were sometimes directed to the Indian mounds to the north of the city, situated on a four-acre plot. Many mounds had been dug away, as the town expanded. They held

---

[89] Latrobe, *The Ramble in North America,* 289.
[90] Davidson, *The Rivers of America,* Vol. 1, 238.
[91] "Rubio,"*Rambles in the United States,* 147.
[92] Cummings, *The Western Pilot* (1829), 50.
[93] "Rubio," *Rambles in the United States,* 147.
[94] Dickens, *American Notes,* 158.
[95] Flagg, *The Far West,* Vol. 2, 115.

artifacts of the Cahokia society, which had flourished until 1200 AD and at one time had numbered twenty thousand inhabitants.

From St. Louis, the two went by steamboat up the Ohio River and debarked at Rockport, where the Gentrys awaited them. The trip had taken three months, but Abe was back home well before seeding, a busy time at the Lincoln homestead. Dutifully, he turned over to his father the twenty-four dollars he had earned from the trip.

Abe returned to his farm duties and to his day labors, but he had caught the steamboat fever. "When I was a boy, there was but one permanent ambition among my comrades," wrote Mark Twain. "That was, to be a steamboatman."[96] Abe expressed interest in finding work aboard a steamboat, but was thwarted by his parental obligation, which continued until his twenty-first birthday. Instead, he turned his interest to the courtroom and attended trials in the nearby county seats, where he observed the prominent attorneys. He read the newspapers that were now being delivered to nearby Gentryville. He listened to the political discussions, and sometimes offered an opinion.

In the autumn of 1829, Thomas Lincoln began to build a new cabin. One cannot be certain of his intent. Probably he meant to entice his stepchildren and their families to remain with him and share in the farm labor. Meanwhile, a devastating "epidemic" of "milk sick" had stricken the Little Pigeon Creek community. John Hanks, a nephew of Nancy Lincoln, who earlier had left for Illinois, sent glowing reports of the healthy, homesteading opportunities in Sangamon County. Dennis Hanks followed him. In one week at Little Pigeon Creek, Dennis had lost four milk cows and eleven

---

[96] Mark Twain [Samuel Clemens], *Life on the Mississippi,* 25.

calves from the "milk sick." Both Hankses announced their intention of moving their families to Illinois. Other relatives concurred, including the families of two of Sarah Bush Lincoln's daughters, who were also living in the Lincoln cabin.

Meanwhile, on February 12, Abe celebrated his twenty-first birthday and became emancipated from paternal control. He made known his intention of leaving home. Since his father realized that he and Sally would be left alone if they remained in Little Pigeon Creek, he yielded to Sally's entreaties and agreed to move to Illinois.

The Little Pigeon Creek community had changed in the fourteen years of the Lincoln sojourn. It had been a wilderness when the family first arrived, but the wilderness had vanished, now transformed into farm country. Hunting was more difficult, quarry scarcer; and the Lincolns were a meat-eating family, increasingly dependant on hogs. The generation that remained would enlarge the tillable acreage, build clapboard houses, install glass windows, build brick chimneys, cultivate orchards, put up bridges; and a few would send their sons to college.[97] People, too, had changed. No longer were they the familiar Kentucky folk who, like the Lincolns, had crossed over the Ohio River. Now, northeasterners were arriving. With the opening of the Erie Canal, people were traveling up the Great Lakes and entering Indiana from the north through the thin remaining strip of Indian land. There were at present forty families in the Little Pigeon Creek neighborhood.

Thomas sold his hundred acres for $125. The distress price was a profound disappointment, but, with the panic of the milk sick epidemic, it was the best that could be obtained. He also sold his wife's property in Elizabethtown for $125

---

[97] Peck, *New Guide for Emigrants,* 119.

and, with the sale of one hundred hogs, four hundred bushels of corn and the public auction ("vandoo") of their chattels, Tom Lincoln left with five hundred dollars in hand. He was leaving, not because he was shiftless and had wanderlust (as is so often stated), but because he foresaw what lay ahead when, without family or kin to rely on, he would grow too old to work. The infirmities of old age appear much earlier in men who perform heavy work, especially those who begin in childhood. Few backwoodsmen escaped disabling arthritis. Besides, there were feuds in the community, and the unlettered Lincolns no longer quite fitted in with the new generation.

At last, preparation for the two-hundred-mile trek was completed. Thirteen people made ready to depart and meet up with the others who were already in Illinois. Three wagons had been built, two drawn by oxen; the third, by horse.

Abe, who had reached his twenty-first birthday, chose to follow along, until his parents could become established in their new homestead. Intellectually, there was little to distinguish him from other young men of his age, apart from a voracious reading appetite, a serviceable handwriting and an ability to reckon fifth-grade proportions. He had some acquaintance with the elements of elocution and could tell stories, almost as good as his father.

The young man laid in a stock of pins, needles, thread and buttons, to peddle along the way. He visited the graves of his mother and sister, to pay his respects. The neighbors gave the families an appropriate send-off, and in March, they hitched up the wagons and left. The party followed the trace for fifty miles to Vincennes, where, for the first time, Abe saw a printing press.[98] Another point of interest in Vincennes was the elegant home of William Henry Harrison ("Old

---

[98] There were many presses in New Orleans.

Tippecanoe"), first territorial governor and later fourteenth President.

Along the way Abe peddled his notions and earned thirty dollars, doubling his investment. The Lincoln party crossed the Wabash River at Vincennes, Indiana, and entered Illinois near present-day Lawrenceville. An old settler trace led them over muddy prairie and through forest. Often, the trace was flooded or covered with a layer of ice. Nights were spent camping.

After a journey of two weeks, they arrived at the Sangamon River, ten miles southwest of present Decatur, and settled on a site atop a bluff, which John Hanks had selected. Wood was plentiful. The men raised a cabin, plowed fifteen acres of prairie land, sowed corn and enclosed the field with a split rail fence. Then Abe announced that he was now on his own. Some fathers give their sons a "freedom suit" when they reach their majority; but Tom did not provide one. His son's attire at the time consisted of a roundabout jacket, waistcoat and breeches, rawhide boots and a sun-bleached felt hat. When summer came, Abe remained in the neighborhood and split rails for other settlers to earn money for material for jeans. He was a good worker and could split four hundred rails in a day.

The first Illinois homestead proved to be a disaster. Autumn brought fever and ague to the Lincoln family, and the winter of 1830-31 was the most severe in memory. Abe almost lost both feet from frostbite. For years to come, people remembered the gigantic snowdrifts. This settled the matter for Thomas.

When spring came, Thomas, Sally and the rest of the clan started back to Indiana, but along the way they stopped off in Coles County, Illinois, where they decided to settle. The men put up a double cabin, which housed eighteen people.

In March 1831, Denton Offut, a promoter with grandiose ideas, hired John Hanks to take a flatboat loaded with farm produce to New Orleans. To fill out the crew, Hanks, himself an experienced boatman, recommended the services of Abe Lincoln and Abe's stepbrother, John Johnson. Each would receive fifty cents a day and a twenty-dollar bonus at the end of the trip. They paddled by canoe down the Sangamon River to Springfield, then just a small river town, where they expected to find the flatboat. Instead, they met Offut, who announced that the crew themselves would have to build the boat.

They cut logs on government land and had them sawed into planks at a nearby mill. With the help of several other men, they constructed an eighty by eighteen-foot flatboat and a dugout canoe. The flatboat was fitted with a plank-and-cloth sail, which subsequently proved of little value.

Construction of the flatboat took four weeks. No sooner had it been launched, when two men who had helped build it, were swept downstream by the current and ended up holding on for dear life to a sunken tree. They were soon joined by another man, who had tried to rescue them. Lincoln attached a line to a log and gave the rope to some people standing on the bank. Riding the log, he maneuvered it to the sawyer and had the three men climb onto it. The current then brought all four safely to shore.

Offut joined the party in April and supervised the loading of the barrels of corn, wheat and pork. They departed somewhat late into the year for a trip down the inland river ways.

On April 19, 1831, the party came to a dam across the Sangamon River at New Salem, no more than a few miles from where the boat was launched. Midway over the milldam, the boat seized and began to ship water. It remained suspended for a day and a night, while the spectators on shore shouted advice. Lincoln had his companions shift the cargo to another boat; then, with an auger borrowed from the nearby coppersmith, he bored a hole in the bottom of the flatboat, to allow water to escape. After plugging the hole, he stationed some onlookers in the prow as ballast; and had the crew catapult the boat over the dam with poles. Years later, he drew on his experience to obtain a patent for aiding boats in a similar predicament by placing bladders below the water line and inflating them with bellows.

Before resuming their journey, Lincoln and Offut visited the settlement atop the hill to survey its prospects. By then, the two-year-old settlement had fifteen houses and a saw and grist mill. Plans were underway for the construction of a score of additional houses, an inn, four stores, a grog shop, a post office, a quarry, a spinning and carding cabin and facilities for the manufacture of shoes, hats, furniture, kegs and barrels. Above all, the village showed promise. Hopes were high that navigation on the Sangamon River would prosper, once the course of the river was straightened and its channel deepened.

Sangamon County now had a population of thousands and was growing fast. Most of the people were of Kentucky origin. The countryside had a gentle roll, and trees were abundant in scattered groves and strips.[99] At the time, Illinois had no cities. Chicago had less than a dozen families; Springfield and Peoria were hamlets.

Offut made arrangements to rent the mill and set up a store in New Salem. Lincoln was invited to clerk for him after the trip, while Offut was building up his business ventures. In his florid imagination, Offut pictured his protégé as the captain of an all-weather steamboat, with rollers to carry it

---

[99] Stuart, *Three Years in North America,* 368.

over obstructions and runners attached to its bottom to negotiate ice.

Offut and his three boatmen departed New Salem in mid-April, 1831. A few miles below town, Lincoln had another opportunity to display his ingenuity. The crew had been trying unsuccessfully to load some hogs onto the flatboat, but the hogs resisted. Lincoln hit on a solution. He had Johnson hold the tail of the hog, while he held the head in an arm-lock and Offut stitched the eyelids. Lincoln could then pick up the hog with his powerful arms and load it onto the boat; after which Offut removed the sutures.

They floated down the Sangamon, patiently dealing with the many obstacles. The river had veered as much as three miles from its former course, and the new channel was loaded with debris. They came to Beardstown, a village with three streets, at the junction of the Illinois River. Some called it "Porkopolis," for its thriving hog export. As the crew struggled to hoist their crude sail, people lining the bank watched them with amusement.

The boat began its slow journey down the Illinois River. This was the route taken by La Salle, who had came south from the Great Lakes. The crew marveled at the broad floodplain of the Illinois River, with its bayous, ponds and swamps. Long willows lined the banks. Blue jays, crows and herons flew overhead. Game was abundant, as were muskrat and even beaver. They fished for catfish, bass, perch and pike and may have sampled the plentiful mussels. An occasional cluster of cabins was seen, but otherwise only tall prairie grass. As they approached the delta, they passed through the Military Bounty Tract, which Congress had reserved for the veterans of the War of 1812.

Finally, they came to the mighty Mississippi River, still a clear waterway. Very soon after, bustling Alton was passed, with its sheltered landing and handsome promenade.[100] The Joliet-Marquette expedition reported having seen some remarkable Indian pictographs on the nearby rock formations. A few miles downriver they viewed the half-mile wide mouth of the challenging Missouri River, where a torrent of turgid waters poured into the Mississippi and continued forty miles downriver before completely blending in. Here began the "American Bottom,"[101] a five-mile-wide strip of fertile bottom land bordering the river, which was said to yield as much as thirty-five bushels of wheat and seventy-five bushels of corn per acre; but was subject to violent and frequent inundation.[102]

St. Louis hove into view. Timber had been cut down around the outskirts, so that prairie was visible. St. Louis now had a population of seven thousand and several hundred houses.[103] The more affluent citizens lived on the higher elevations.

A dozen steamboats lined the quay, tied up alongside the limestone warehouses. Miners, trappers, adventurers and emigrants roamed the streets. The English language now dominated, but French was still spoken by many. Commerce had begun to boom. Goods could now be shipped to St. Louis more cheaply through the Erie Canal and the Great Lakes than by way of New Orleans. Wrote one enthusiastic traveler: "If there is a place in the whole of the American Union that bids fair for permanent prosperity, it is this St. Louis."[104]

John Hanks left the party at St. Louis. Their late departure had interrupted his schedule, and he was needed back home in time for sowing. Hanks paid six cents to cross the river by

---

[100] Flag, *The Far West,* Vol. 2, 66.

[101] Latrobe, *The Ramble in North America,* 237.

[102] Parker, *A Trip to the West and Texas,* 97.

[103] Stuart, *Three Years in North America,* 314.

[104] "Rubio," *Rambles in the United States,* 143.

steam ferryboat[105] and walked back to Decatur. The other three continued on.

Below St. Louis, the width of the river narrowed and its level dropped four inches every mile all the way to the Gulf of Mexico. They floated by small villages, built near the lead mines. St. Genevieve Island appeared, surrounded by wood rafts. The old town of St. Genevieve had grown to fifteen hundred inhabitants but retained its French flavor. In its vicinity were iron and copper mines. The "American Bottom," which had begun at Alton, ended here. Inland lay rich prairie. On the Missouri side, "they passed Grand Tower," a perpendicular limestone column 150 feet high. Across the river were other noteworthy stone formations, each with a different name.[106]

Many screw wheels floated on the surface of the river,[107] which had to be carefully avoided. These were connected by a long shaft to the gears of nearby millhouses. Deer swam in the river. After a long succession of islands, they came to Cape Girardeau up on the heights, another old French settlement, which had suffered damage in the Great Earthquake. Farmland extended into the interior as far as the eye could see. An interminable succession of islands was passed. Fifty miles below Cape Girardeau, they came to an ox-bow bend of the Mississippi, which heralded its junction with the Ohio River.

Cummings cautioned the boatman to take the "channel to the right; incline well over to the right, opposite No. 1 [island] and when past it, keep to the left again."[108] At the mouth of the Ohio, the Mississippi was more than a mile wide.

---

[105] Stuart, *Three Years in North America,* 317.

[106] George Conclin, *Conclin's New River Guide,* 70; Flagg, *The Far West,* Vol. 2, 59.

[107] Flagg, *The Far West,* Vol. 2, 57.

[108] Cummings, *The Western Pilot* (1829), 58.

Cairo sat at the confluence of the Ohio and Mississippi Rivers. Here, in an earlier geologic time, the Mississippi entered the Gulf of Mexico, but sedimentation and time had pushed the Gulf further south.[109]

Boats plying the two rivers often put into Cairo. The town was strategically located, but repeated inundations had discouraged development. Although in dry weather the town was thirty feet above water, Cairo could be ten feet below, after a season of freshets.[110] Wrote the dour Charles Dickens of Cairo: "a breeding place of fever, ague and death, on which the half-built houses rot away."[111]

Having now come onto what was called "the lower Mississippi," the crew noticed that the steamer (rudder) "bit" better in the fast current, making steering easier. Islands went by so numerous that many had numbers instead of names. Sixty miles below Cairo, on an ox-bow turn of the Mississippi River, they came to Island Ten, outside of New Madrid. The island would later be remembered as a Confederate citadel. New Madrid offered little incentive to go ashore. The Cummings guide warned the voyager: "There is a very large bar round the left hand point above New Madrid; channel near the right shore for nearly four miles above and below New Madrid."[112]

Down the Mississippi they floated. Steamboat passengers waved to them from the cabin deck. They passed flatboats laden with barrels of pork, kegs of lard, hogsheads of tobacco, bags of corn and bars of lead.[113] Steamboats went by carrying chicken coops, horses, men, slaves, gamblers, horse jockeys,

---

[109] Price, *The Amazing Mississippi,* 3.
[110] Parker, *A Trip to the West,* 107.
[111] Ibid., 111.
[112] Cummings, *The Western Pilot* (1829), 59.
[113] Parker, *A Trip to the West,* 111.

slave dealers, and women of ill repute. Towards dusk, they put in to shore, braving the insects, which left them with swollen faces and eyelids. To travel at night would have been an unacceptable risk.

Over the evening meal, they argued politics. Tom Lincoln, John and Dennis Hanks and most of Little Pigeon Creek, were all Jackson Democrats, overjoyed that the New England elite and the "Virginia Dynasty" had been turned out of office. All five Indiana electoral votes had gone to Andrew Jackson. Offut, on the other hand, came from Lexington Kentucky, the home of Senator Henry Clay, the Whig leader, who promised canals, internal improvements and commercial expansion. Few could better the glib Denton Offut in an argument.

They saw a succession of bluffs on the Tennessee side. On the fourth bluff, lay the rapidly growing town of Memphis, built on the site of old Fort Pickering. The guide informed riverboat men that the town is "healthy and advantageously situated for trade… [It] bids fair to become an important place of business."[114]

They tied up at Memphis, Tennessee, and remained for the day. A guard could be posted, while the others inspected the town atop the bluffs. Since Lincoln's last trip, the status of the Indian nations had changed. No sooner had Andrew Jackson taken office as President, when the states of Mississippi and Alabama refused to further recognize Cherokee, Chickasaw and Choctaw sovereignties, presaging their expulsion to the Indian (Oklahoma) Territory.

Although Andrew Jackson held that the power to regulate the tribes was vested in the states, he used his authority as President to accelerate their expulsion. Even before he was

---

[114] Cummings , *The Western Pilot* (1829), 61.

elected to the presidency, he pressured the Cherokee to sell land. Later, when a decision of the Supreme Court favored the nations, he refused to execute the decision. In time, he would provide troops to effect the expulsion, not only from the states east of the Mississippi River, but as well from Arkansas.

Plantations were growing briskly in the delta. Slaves were being brought from the east, where the cotton fields were rapidly loosing their fertility. In Virginia, the annual cotton production had slumped from twenty-five million to ten million pounds. Virginia now "exported" six thousand slaves a year, and slaves now accounted for half the assessed value of Virginia real estate.

South of Memphis, they began to see an almost continuous line of plantations with long rows of negro huts.[115] On the west bank of Arkansas, the band of settlement was thicker, but there were few towns. They passed fourteen or more islands and came to the mouth of the White River, where huge catfish could be caught, even by hand. Settlement had followed the White River northward deep into the Arkansas Territory. A few hours later, they reached the junction with the Arkansas River. The Arkansas River was second only to the Missouri River in length, flowing two thousand miles from the Rockies. Once again, farmsteads had followed the Arkansas River, all the way up to Fort Smith, on the border of the Indian Territory. Settlers squatted on land along the banks, hoping to have first claim under the preemption law when the government authorized settlement.[116]

Islands 75-103 were passed, and they came to Vicksburg, where they made a short stop. Offut was less interested in trading than of reaching New Orleans, where he hoped to

---

[115] Henry Tudor, *Narrative of a Tour in North America,* Vol. 2, 61.
[116] Peck, *A New Guide for Emigrants,* 119; Stuart, *Three Years in North America,* 265.

explore the commercial possibilities. The thick loamy soil around Vicksburg was yielding a good crop of cotton, grain and tobacco, but, again, the bounty mostly seemed to be benefiting the larger holdings. The Choctaw Nation still had tenuous possession of their land, but premonitions of their removal across the Mississippi were unmistakable.

Below Vicksburg, they passed four islands and several bayous. When they looked up, Natchez loomed ahead, perched atop its bluff. They may have heard the saying: "Memphis the most pleasant town, Vicksburg the most flourishing and Natchez the largest."[117] At Natchez, they made another short stop. Since Lincoln's last visit, Natchez had grown to fifteen hundred people, but it was only a small town with handsome houses. Hundreds of flatboats were tied up along the landing, and the streets of Under-The-Hill were crowded with "boatmen, malattos, houses of ill-fame and their wretched tenants." It was still "the resort of all that is vile," [118] but worth a quick look.

As they moved south into Louisiana, they began to see villas with gardens of orange trees and evergreen shrubs. Great blue kingfishers flew overhead and black and grey squirrels peered at them from the shore. South of Natchez, they approached a long bend, where the Red River enters. Within the year, a "cut-off" would short-circuit the bend and permit a more direct route, allowing the boatman to avoid an encounter with the "Great Raft."

The next day they came to Baton Rouge. Here, the levee commenced on both sides of the river and continued 125 miles south to New Orleans. Sugar plantations were flourishing. With adequate slave labor, five acres could produce five thousand pounds of sugar and 125 gallons of molasses. Surely,

[117] A. Parker, *A Trip To the West,* 123.
[118] Cummings, *The Western Pilot* (1829), 70.

as they passed it, Lincoln pointed out Madame Duchesne's plantation, where he and Allen Gentry had been attacked.

After another two days of expectant journey, New Orleans finally came into view. The trip had taken somewhat more than a month. They arrived in May, comfortably before the beginning of the yellow fever season,[119] when the city took on the name of "the wet grave."[120] No one can remain in the district after July, cautioned one traveler.[121] They floated past the crowded boating and tied up two miles below the city.

The three men remained for a month in New Orleans. Offut sold cargo and boat, then began to scout the city for commercial opportunities. He sought to establish a line of credit, so that he could buy *en gros* quantities of Illinois produce, as jobbers do for cotton. Without such arrangements, his purchases would be limited to cash transactions, since credit back home was scarce.

Offut visited many of the branch houses of the principle banks and brokers of Europe and the North. Perhaps, as he made his rounds, he took Lincoln with him, although it is not likely that a shabbily dressed, young boatman would greatly enhance his image. Cotton transactions were conducted in a frenzy, as thousands of bales daily exchanged hands. They heard the thumping of the cotton presses, which compacted cotton to half its original volume at a cost seventy-five cents per bale, greatly reducing the cost of transshipment.[122] Offut spent weeks trying to establish a line of credit, apparently to no avail.

Meanwhile, the crew had ample time to explore the city. They wandered the narrow cobbled streets and watched the

---

[119] "Rubio," *Rambles in the United States,* 148.
[120] Latrobe, *The Ramble in North America,* Vol. 2, 330.
[121] "Rubio," *Rambles in the United States,* 148.
[122] Parker, *A Trip to the West,* 229.

celebrations of strange festivals. Draymen crowded the market, moving recklessly through the throng. Clusters of mulatto women sat on mats, with heads covered by bright kerchiefs and shoulders wrapped in rabbit skin shawls. They offered for sale bananas, plantains, oranges, exotic fruits, cocoa, unfamiliar fish laid out on palmetto leaves and a variety of eggs wrapped in Spanish moss.[123] Offut and the crew carefully noted the salient prices: pork, three dollars a hundred-weight; bacon, ten to twelve cents per pound; hogs, two dollars a head.[124]

The traveler surely would not fail to visit the famous battleground, now pastureland, six miles south of the city, where in 1814, Andrew Jackson and his three thousand irregulars defeated a mighty British army four times its size, including the regiment that had burned Washington to the ground!

Most unforgettable of all for Lincoln were the visits to the slave auctions. Stripped to the waist, women were handled, paraded up and down and made to submit to examinations of their mouths and other parts, to insure no infirmity. Both sexes were pinched, inspected, manhandled and trotted, to the amusement or indifference of onlookers. Children were beaten to separate them from the clutching arms of their parents and sold off to different buyers. All this Lincoln witnessed with a feeling of disbelief, horror and helplessness.

Finally, the time came for their return. Offut took great care in selecting the steamboat. Since accidents were frequent, the prudent traveler made thorough inquiry into the reputation of the captain and his steamboat.

In June 1831, they boarded a steamboat bound for St. Louis. What travel arrangement Offut made for himself is not

---

[123] Latrobe, *The Ramble in North America,* Vol. 2, 332.
[124] [author not given] *Remarks on the Western States of America,* 39.

known, but there can be no doubt that his crew traveled on the top deck. The trip took a week. Once in St. Louis, Offut remained behind to purchase stock for his new store in New Salem. Lincoln and his stepbrother crossed by steam ferryboat to Edwardsville, Illinois, and returned on foot to the Lincoln homestead, now in Coles County, Illinois. There, he stayed for one month and helped his parents settle in. Doubtless, he spent many hours recounting the details of his recent trip. The Coles County home was the second of Thomas Lincoln's four homesteads in Illinois.

Abe left home with little regret. The crowding of all eighteen quasi-illiterates in their double log cabin, the pervading body odors, the flatulence, the children's cries, the reek of babies' wastes and the stench of the overused privy were recollections he was pleased to forget, now that he had seen in his travels other modes of living.

Abe Lincoln set out for New Salem and arrived there in July 1831, in time to offer his services as an assistant clerk in a local election and to take an oath to support the Constitution of the United States.

A few days after the election, Lincoln again found employment as a riverboat man. One of the New Salem citizens had decided to emigrate to Texas. He had had a flatboat built and loaded onto it his chattels and dunnage. Lincoln, who was regarded as a skilled riverboat man, was hired to take the flatboat down the Sangamon River to Beardstown. Since it was August and low water, the job was both challenging and fatiguing. Lincoln succeeded in bringing the flatboat safely to Beardstown, where he was replaced. He was paid off and walked back to New Salem.

In March of the following year, Lincoln was again employed as a river man.[125] The steamboat *Talisman* had departed Cincinnati and traveled down the Ohio, past the falls and up the Illinois River to Beardstown; then up the Sangamon River by way of New Salem to Springfield. The journey was meant to demonstrate the feasibility of navigating the Sangamon by steamboat. According to Lincoln, the *Talisman* was unique, in that it had "a five-foot boiler and a nine-foot whistle and every time the whistle blew, the boat stopped."

In preparation for the boat's arrival, Lincoln and the other townsmen cleared the Sangamon of its many snags and obstacles. The *Talisman* was able to negotiate the dam at New Salem, then proceed to the head of navigation, five miles from Springfield. There it lingered for many weeks, while the captain basked in the public plaudits. Meanwhile, the weather had changed, and the high water had receded. The captain anticipated difficulties on the return trip, and was told of a knowledgeable river man, who had greatly impressed the townspeople of New Salem the year before. He hired Lincoln to help bring the vessel to Beardstown. Progress was slow; the *Talisman* traveled no more than four miles a day. One may be sure that although Lincoln was hired as pilot, he worked hard with the others at removing the obstacles along the way. At New Salem, part of the dam had to be removed before the boat could pass.[126] The young pilot brought the boat safely to Beardstown and was paid forty dollars for his services, which was three times the pay of a boatman for the three week's work. Sadly, the tribulations of the *Talisman* had clearly demonstrated that the Sangamon River was unsuited for extensive steamboat navigation. Thenceforth, the prospects of

---

[125] William H. Herndon and Jesse Weik, *Herndon's Lincoln*, 88-91.
[126] Paul Horgon, *Citizen of New Salem*, 35.

New Salem dimmed. Later, an attempt would be made to bring another steamboat, the *Utility*, up the Sangamon River to New Salem. It did, in fact, arrive below the dam but could not return, since the water was near low level. The steamboat rotted away at New Salem and was later broken up.

Lincoln lived for six years in New Salem. During this time, he studied grammar, mathematics, surveying, politics, debating and other subjects. He acquired a rudimentary knowledge of military evolutions and captained a company of rag-tag volunteers for ninety days. Some say he had a deep romance with an auburn-haired girl, but a year after her death, we find him unenthusiastically courting the rather unattractive Mary Owens. Here in New Salem, he began the study of the law and prepared himself for a political career.

But there can be no doubt that life on the waterways had left its mark on the outlook of the ever-searching Abe Lincoln.

Deep in study in New Salem.
[Lincoln Museum, Ft. Wayne, #315.]

SELECT BIBLIOGRAPHY

Ambler, Charles Henry. *A History of Transportation in the Ohio Valley*. Westport, CT: Greenwood Press, 1931.

Barton, William E. *The Life of Abraham Lincoln*. Indianapolis: Bobbs Merrill, 1925.

Bullock, W. *Sketch of a Journey*. London: Miller, 1827 Microfilm NYPL XBB-110).

Clark, Thomas D. *Frontier America*. New York: Scribner, 1959.

Clemens, Samuel [Mark Twain]. *Life on the Mississippi*. New York: Signet, 2001.

Cummings, Samuel. *The Western Pilot*. Cincinnati, 1829, 34, Cincinnati: Guilford, 1829.

Conclin, George. *Conclin's New River Guide*. Cincinnati: Conclin, 1849.

Daniels, Jonathan. *The Devil's Backbone*. New York, Toronto, London: McGraw-Hill, 1962.

Davidson, Donald. *The Rivers of America*. Vol. 1. New York, Toronto: Rinehart, 1947.

Dickens, Charles. *American Notes*. New York: St. Martin's Press, 1985.

Dunbar, Seymour. *A History of Travel in America,* New York: Tudor Publishing, 1937.

Faragher, John Mack. *Daniel Boone*. New York: Holt, 1992.

Flagg, Edmund. *The Far West*. New York: Harper and Brothers, 1838.

Flint, Timothy. *Recollections of the Last Ten Years*. Boston: Cummings, Hilliard, 1826.

Hall, (no first name). *Letters from the West*. London: Colburn, 1828.

Hartley, Cecil B. *The Life of Daniel Boone*. New York: A.L. Burt, [no date].

Hawgood, John. *America's Western Frontier*. New York: Knopf, 1967.

Horgon, Paul. *Citizen of New Salem*. New York: Ferrar, Straus & Cudahy, 1961.

James, Thomas Horton ["Rubio"]. *Rambles in the United States and Canada*. London: Samuel Clark, 1846.

Johnson, Leland R. *The Falls City Engineers, A History of the Louisville District Corps of Engineers,* Chap. II. *Ohio River Navigation 1783-1824,* U.S. Army, December 24, 1974 in http://www.usace.army.mil/publications/misc/un22/toc.htm.

Lamon, Ward H. *The Life of Abraham Lincoln*. Boston: Osgood, 1872.

Latrobe, Charles Joseph. *The Ramble in North America*. London: Seeley and Burnside, 1836.

McDougall, Walter A. *Freedom Just around the Corner*. New York: Harper Collins, 2004.

[author not given]. *Remarks on the Western States of America*. London: Kennett, 1830.

Parker, A.A. *A Trip to the West and Texas.* Concord, N.H.: William White; Boston: Mussey, 1836.

Peck, J.M. *New Guide for Emigrants to the West.* Boston: Gould, Kendall & Lincoln, 1834.

Price, Willard. *The Amazing Mississippi.* New York: John Day, 1963.

Reep, Thomas P. *Lincoln at New Salem*, Old Salem Lincoln League, 1927.

Riegel, Robert and Robert Athearn. *America Moves West.* New York & Chicago: Holt, Rinehart and Winston, 1966.

Sandburg, Carl. *The Prairie Years,* Vol. 1. New York: Harcourt, Brace & Co., 1926.

Stern, Philip Van Doren. *The Life and Writings of Abraham Lincoln.* New York: Random House, 1940.

Stuart, James. *Three Years in North America.* Edinburgh: Robert Cadell, 1838.

Thomas, Benjamin P. *Abraham Lincoln.* New York: Knopf,1953

Thwaites, R. G. *Afloat on the Ohio.* Chicago: Way and Williams, 1897.

Tudor, Henry. *Narrative of a Tour in North America.* Vol. 2. London: James Duncan, 1834.

[no author]. *Remarks on the Western States of America.* London: Kennett, 1830.

Warren, Louis A. *Lincoln's youth.* Indianapolis, Indiana: Indiana Historical Society, 1959.

INDEX

About the Author

Dr. J. C. Ladenheim is a retired neurosurgeon and student of nineteenth-century American history. His recent books, *Alien Horseman* and *Custer's Thorn*, both published by Heritage Books, deal with the Custer saga. His forthcoming *The Jarrett-Palmer Transcontinental Express of 1876* describes the little-known three-day cross-country train trip.

www.ingramcontent.com/pod-product-compliance
Lightning Source LLC
LaVergne TN
LVHW051707080426
835511LV00017B/2774